Entering God's Rest

Entering God's Rest

by
John MacArthur, Jr.

WORD OF GRACE COMMUNICATIONS
P.O. Box 4000
Panorama City, CA 91412

All Scripture quotations, unless noted otherwise, are from the *New Scofield Reference Bible,* King James Version. Copyright © 1967 by Oxford University Press, Inc. Reprinted by permission.

Library of Congress Cataloging in Publication Data

MacArthur, John F.
  Entering God's rest.

  (John MacArthur's Bible studies)
  Includes indexes.
  1. Bible. N.T. Hebrews III, I-IV, 16—Criticism, interpretation, etc. I. Title. II. Series: MacArthur, John F. Bible studies.
BS2775.2.M3   1987   227'.8706   87-3403
ISBN 0-8024-5316-3

1 2 3 4 5 6 7 Printing/LC/Year 91 90 89 88 87

Printed in the United States of America

Contents

These Bible studies are taken from messages delivered by Pastor-Teacher John MacArthur, Jr., at Grace Community Church in Panorama City, California. These messages have been combined into a 4-tape album entitled *Entering God's Rest.* You may purchase this series either in an attractive vinyl cassette album or as individual cassettes. To purchase these tapes, request the album *Entering God's Rest*, or ask for the tapes by their individual GC numbers. Please consult the current price list; then, send your order, making your check payable to:

WORD OF GRACE COMMUNICATIONS
P.O. Box 4000
Panorama City, CA 91412

Or call the following number:
818-982-7000

1
Jesus, Greater Than Moses

Outline

Introduction
A. The Addressees
    1. Weak believers
    2. Intellectually convinced unbelievers
    3. Unconvinced unbelievers
B. The Announcement

Lesson
I. Jesus Is Superior in His Office (v. 1)
    A. The Terms
       1. "Wherefore"
       2. "Holy brethren"
       3. "Partakers of the heavenly calling"
       4. "Consider"
          a) Its importance
          b) Its illustrations
             (1) 2 Timothy 2
             (2) Hebrews 12
    B. The Titles
       1. Apostle
       2. High Priest
II. Jesus Is Superior in His Works (vv. 2-4)
    A. His Similarity to Moses
       1. The statement of faithfulness
          a) Regarding Jesus
          b) Regarding Moses
       2. The sphere of faithfulness
          a) Moses in his household
          b) Christ in His household
    B. His Difference from Moses

7

III. Jesus Is Superior in His Person (vv. 5-6)
   A. The Servant
   B. The Shadow
   C. The Son
   D. The Security
      1. The problem
      2. The passages

Conclusion

Introduction

A. The Addressees

The book of Hebrews was written to a community of Jewish people located outside the Jerusalem area. They had been evangelized by the apostles and prophets, and some had believed. Some were intellectually convinced but had never made the step of faith. Others had never been convinced; they had heard the gospel but had not responded to it. The letter to the Hebrews addresses all three groups, and in each context it is necessary to determine which group is being addressed to interpret the passage correctly.

1. Weak believers

Those who had received Christ were put out of the synagogue, ostracized from Jewish society, and persecuted relentlessly. Because of the persecution, their faith was weak, and they tended to hold onto the rituals of the Old Covenant. Paul exhorted a similar group in Galatia to "stand fast, therefore, in the liberty with which Christ hath made us free, and be not entangled again with the yoke of bondage [to the Old Covenant]" (Gal. 5:1). Although in the New Covenant there is freedom in Christ, they had not begun to experience it; they were still struggling with legalism. They were weaker brothers, like those Paul wrote of in Romans 14. The writer of Hebrews wanted to strengthen their faith and show them they could stop clinging to the outward rituals of the Old Covenant. Christ was sufficient for their needs under the New Covenant.

2. Intellectually convinced unbelievers

The intellectually convinced unbelievers were warned to act on the truth they heard lest they fall away and never come to repentance. Because they knew the truth but willfully rejected it, the strong warning of Hebrews 10:29 is addressed to them: "Of how much sorer punishment, suppose ye, shall he be thought worthy, who hath trodden under foot the Son of God, and hath counted the blood of the covenant, with which he was sanctified, an unholy thing, and hath done despite unto the Spirit of grace?"

3. Unconvinced unbelievers

The unconvinced unbelievers were not convinced of the truth of Christianity. The gospel is presented to them several times in the book of Hebrews.

B. The Announcement

The message to all three groups is the supremacy of Christ. The message to believers who are hanging onto the Old Covenant is that the New Covenant brought by Christ is superior. The message to intellectually convinced unbelievers is that Christ is sufficient. And the message to unconvinced unbelievers is that Christ is supreme.

To prove that the New Covenant is superior to the Old Covenant, it is necessary to show that Christ is superior to all those connected with the Old Covenant. The writer of Hebrews proves that Jesus is superior to angels (chaps. 1-2), Moses (chap. 3), Joshua (chap. 4), the Aaronic priesthood (chap. 7), and the Old Testament sacrifices (chaps. 10-11). The theme of the book of Hebrews is summed up in Hebrews 3:1: consider Jesus. It is important for all men of all ages to consider Jesus. In chapter 3 the writer urges his readers to consider Jesus as he compares Him to Moses.

Lesson

To understand verses 1-6, which are the doctrinal foundation for the exhortation beginning in verse 7, we need to know something about Moses. If we're to understand why Jesus is better than Moses, we must know a little bit about who Moses was. The Jewish people held Moses in high esteem. In fact, he is the most highly regarded figure in their history. He was the man to whom God spoke face to face (Ex. 33:11). Moses saw the glory of God (Ex. 33:18-23), and the glow on his face reflected that fact (Ex. 34:30). He was the man God chose to lead Israel out of Egypt. But most significant of all to the Jewish people was that through Moses came the law. In fact, the law became so identified with Moses that it was commonly referred to as the law of Moses. The law was the heart of Jewish life; the Old Testament commandments and rituals were given the highest priority. Paul mentions in Romans 2 that the Jews boasted in the law. Moses had not only given them the Ten Commandments, but he had penned the entire Pentateuch. Some Jews believed that Moses was greater than the angels.

Moses led a remarkable life. The hand of God preserved him as a baby and dug his grave after his death. In between those two points in his life were numerous miracles. During the most memorable times of Israel's history it was Moses whom God worked through. It was Moses who led the children of Israel out of Egypt. It was Moses who led them through the wilderness. It was Moses who instructed them from the mouth of God. The whole Levitical system came through Moses. It was Moses who gave the plans for the Tabernacle, the Ark of the Covenant, and everything that went with it. As great as Moses was, however, the Holy Spirit in this section calls on us to gaze on Jesus, who is far greater than Moses.

The writer of Hebrews presents three areas in which Jesus is superior to Moses:

I. JESUS IS SUPERIOR IN HIS OFFICE (v. 1)

"Wherefore, holy brethren, partakers of the heavenly calling, consider the Apostle and High Priest of our profession, Christ Jesus."

A. The Terms

1. "Wherefore"

"Wherefore" indicates the writer is building on something he has said before this verse; it points backwards. We are to consider Jesus because of what the writer has just said about Him. In chapter 2 we read that Jesus was made lower than the angels (v. 9), is the captain of our salvation (v. 10), is the One who sanctifies us (v. 11), and is the One who calls us His brethren (v. 12). Jesus destroyed Satan and death (v. 14), thus delivering us from bondage (v. 15). He is powerful, sympathetic, merciful, and faithful (vv. 16-18).

The writer of Hebrews is speaking to Jews who believed in Christ but were still clinging to the outward forms of the Old Covenant. He urges them to focus on the absolute sufficiency of Jesus. They can drop the trappings and rituals of the Old Covenant; they are no longer needed. They have a new High Priest sent from God. That was an important message for them to hear.

Leaving the Past Behind

Most of us can't understand the difficulties the Hebrew Christians faced in coming out of Judaism; we find it difficult to understand why they were tempted to hang onto their old way of life. Even today it can be difficult for a Jewish believer to make the break with Judaism. However, I think everyone finds it hard to let go of the idea that his works and his religious trappings are necessary to please God. And while Christians accept God's free grace in Christ, many tend to hang onto an artificial legalism rather than living the positive, Christ-controlled, Spirit-energized life. The statements of Christ's sufficiency shatter all legalistic efforts, whether those of first-century Judaism or twentieth-century Protestantism.

2. "Holy brethren"

Many people claim the entire book of Hebrews is addressed to believers, since the author uses the word

11

brethren. However, that word is sometimes used in the New Testament to refer to unsaved Jews (e.g., Acts 2:29; 13:38). When the writer of Hebrews wished to make clear he was speaking to believers, he used the term "holy brethren." Only believers are holy brethren, since they are Christ's brethren (Heb. 2:11). Therefore this passage is addressed to Christians.

Believers are sanctified—set apart and made holy in Christ at salvation. Hebrews 10:10 says, "We are sanctified [made holy] through the offering of the body of Jesus Christ once for all." Verse 14 says, "For by one offering He hath perfected forever them that are sanctified [made holy]." Verses 17-18 say, "Their sins and iniquities will I remember no more. Now where remission of these is, there is no more offering for sin." Because the believer's sin was removed at the cross by virtue of his position in Christ, there is no more need for a sin offering.

3. "Partakers of the heavenly calling"

Many of the promises of the Old Covenant concerned earthly blessings, such as inheriting the land God promised. Christianity is a spiritual and heavenly calling with a spiritual and heavenly inheritance. As Paul says in Philippians 3:20, "Our citizenship is in heaven, from which also we look for the Savior, the Lord Jesus Christ." Our home is in heaven, and we are citizens of God's realm, the heavenly places (Eph. 1:3). We're only strangers and pilgrims here (1 Pet. 2:11). We are in the world but not of the world (John 17:11, 16).

That is a powerful point for Jewish believers who were still clinging to the rituals of the Old Covenant. The writer exhorts them to let go of earthly things since their citizenship is in heaven. There is no point in hanging ontothe earthly ritual once they have the heavenly reality.

4. "Consider"

   a) Its importance

   "Consider" means to set your mind on something or to focus intently. Some may wonder why the writer tells Christians to consider Christ, since we already know Him. But believers are a long way from understanding all that Christ is. Even the apostle Paul did not know all that he wanted to about Christ (Phil. 3:10). When trials or temptations come into our lives, we need to focus our attention on Jesus and keep it there until all that He is begins to unfold for us. Many Christians are spiritually weak and struggle with worry and anxiety because they don't know the depths and the riches of Christ. Jesus promised rest for our souls when we learn of Him (Matt. 11:29). Do you really enjoy your Christian life? Is it exciting? That's how it ought to be. Does the fellowship and presence of Jesus Christ thrill you? If not, perhaps you don't know Him as well as you might.

Learning to Appreciate the Masters

When I was in college I would go to downtown Los Angeles and pay fifty cents to hear the Philharmonic orchestra rehearse. I would take a couple books with me and sit up in the balcony, listening to a concert while I did homework. I listened to the works of Bartók, Moussorgsky's *Pictures at an Exhibition,* and other classical compositions. I enjoyed myself and began to appreciate the masters. However, some people hear that style of music and say, "That stuff is too dull!" Some go to an art gallery to see the works of the masters and say, "Who cares? I'm bored!" Such people need to learn to appreciate the masters. It's important to cultivate a love for good music and good art. We need to recognize beauty, genius, and virtue (Phil. 4:8). The same is true of our spiritual lives. If you want to enjoy Jesus Christ, you need to stay with Him until you learn how, until your Christian life is filled with joy.

b) Its illustrations

(1) 2 Timothy 2

Timothy was having problems. He was young, and he was being harassed by people in Ephesus who were teaching false doctrine. People were criticizing him, and he became discouraged. He may even have been developing an ulcer, since Paul advised him to take a little wine for the sake of his stomach. Paul exhorted him to stay with it—to be like a good soldier, a hard-working farmer, and a well-trained athlete. His main point is in verse 8, "Remember Jesus Christ, risen from the dead, descendant of David, according to my gospel" (NASB*) The most important thing Timothy needed to do in the midst of all his problems was to remember Jesus Christ.

(2) Hebrews 12

Verses 1-2 read, "Wherefore, seeing we also are compassed about with so great a cloud of witnesses, let us lay aside every weight, and the sin which doth so easily beset us, and let us run with patience the race that is set before us, looking unto Jesus." When we run the Christian race, we need to focus on Jesus. I used to run the 100-yard dash and the 220 in college. One thing I learned was that you can't run and watch your feet at the same time. When you run, just like when you drive, you need to set your sights on something in the distance. When we ran sprints we used to keep our eyes on the tape at the finish line. Not only did that motivate us, but it also kept us going in the right direction. In the Christian race, if we have our eyes on ourselves we will run into wall after wall. We need to keep our eyes fixed on "the author and the finisher of our faith" (Heb. 12:2). He is the goal of the Christian race.

New American Standard Bible.

B. The Titles

Jesus is better than Moses in that He is both an Apostle and High Priest. Moses was not. Moses was an apostle in the sense that he was sent by God, but Aaron was the high priest.

1. Apostle

An apostle (Gk., *apostolos*) is a messenger or ambassador. Jesus is the supreme ambassador from God sent to earth. An ambassador represents all the power and authority of the government that sends him. Jesus represents the power, justice, grace, love, and mercy of God. An ambassador also speaks with the voice of the one who sent him. That was true of Jesus, who said, "I have not spoken of myself; but the Father, who sent me, he gave me a commandment, what I should say, and what I should speak" (John 12:49).

2. High Priest

Jesus is our High Priest, the supreme mediator between God and man. He brings God and man together.

So as Hebrews 3:1 says, Jesus is "the Apostle and High Priest of our profession." The writer is telling the believing Jews that since they have confessed Jesus as their Lord, they certainly ought to gaze on Him. Too many Christians have confessed Jesus Christ as Savior and Lord yet still run the Christian race without looking at Him.

II. JESUS IS SUPERIOR IN HIS WORKS (vv. 2-4)

"Who was faithful to him that appointed him, as also Moses was faithful in all his house. For this man was counted worthy of more glory than Moses, inasmuch as he who hath built the house hath more honor than the house. For every house is built by some man, but he that built all things is God."

A. His Similarity to Moses

Since Moses was so highly esteemed by the Jewish people, the writer of Hebrews doesn't just bluntly state that Jesus is greater than Moses. He handles the matter more delicately. Before taking up Jesus' superiority to Moses, He points out the resemblance between the two.

1. The statement of faithfulness

   a) Regarding Jesus

   The first part of verse 2 tells us that Jesus was faithful to God. Jesus did the work that the Father appointed Him to do. In John 6:38-39 He says, "I came down from heaven, not to do mine own will but the will of him that sent me. And this is the Father's will who hath sent me, that of all that he hath given me I should lose nothing, but should raise it up again at the last day." Jesus says in John 7:18, "He that speaketh of himself seeketh his own glory; but he that seeketh his glory that sent him, the same is true, and no unrighteousness is in him." In John 8:29 He says, "He that sent me is with me. The Father hath not left me alone; for I do always those things that please him," while in John 17:4-5 we read, "I have finished the work which thou gavest me to do. And now, O Father, glorify thou me with thine own self with the glory which I had with thee before the world was." Jesus always did the Father's will. He was ever faithful.

   b) Regarding Moses

   The last half of verse 2 speaks of the faithfulness of Moses: "As also Moses was faithful in all his house." That thought comes from Numbers 12:7, where God speaks of Moses "who is faithful in all mine house." He led the children of Israel out of Egypt. He believed God, and God performed great miracles through him, such as the parting of the Red Sea. He faithfully led the children of Israel during their forty years of wandering in the wilderness. Although there were times when Moses was unfaithful, such as when he killed an Egyptian, or when he struck a rock instead of speaking to it as he was told, faithfulness was the overall pattern of his life.

2. The sphere of faithfulness

   a) Moses in his household

   The word translated "house" (Gk., *oikos*) refers to an entire household. Moses was a faithful steward over God's household. (The household of God in the Old Testament was the Old Testament believers: Israel and the Gentile proselytes.) A steward does not own the house—he manages it for the owner. God owned the house of Israel, and Moses managed it. He was in charge of dispensing the truths that God committed to his trust, and he was faithful to do so.

   b) Christ in His household

   Ephesians 2:19 tells us what Christ's household is: "Ye are no more strangers and sojourners, but fellow citizens with the saints, and of the household of God" (cf. 1 Pet. 2:4-5). The household of God here is a reference to the church. Believers in the Old Testament were the household of Moses, and believers of the New Testament are the household of Christ. Just as Moses was faithful to an earthly household, Jesus was faithful to a heavenly household. Like Moses, Christ was and is faithful to minister to His household.

Are You a Faithful Steward?

We are all stewards in God's house, though in a lesser sense than Jesus. All of us have spiritual gifts that God has entrusted to us for the edification of others (Rom. 12:3-8; 1 Cor. 12:4-31; Eph. 4:7-16; 1 Pet. 4:10-11). If you're unfaithful in ministering your spiritual gifts, you're being an unfaithful steward. You are responsible to make Christ known by witnessing to the people God has placed around you, and perhaps you've been unfaithful in doing that. Some of you have been given a position of teaching, but you've not been faithful to study diligently and sacrificially. That's being an unfaithful steward. The Christian life is a sacred trust given to you by God, and it demands your faithfulness. The greatest thrill I could ever imagine would be to have someone say at the end of my life, "As Jesus was faithful to the Father, so was John MacArthur." That may sound presumptuous—I'm not in the same class with Jesus —yet it was said of Moses in verse 2. I don't think we've begun to discover what God can do through us if we're willing to be faithful.

B. His Difference from Moses

Although Moses and Jesus were both faithful, there was a difference. In verse 3 we read that Jesus "was counted worthy of more glory than Moses, inasmuch as he who hath built the house hath more honor than the house." Moses was but a member of the spiritual household that Jesus built. Jesus created both Israel and the church. That is evidence of His deity, since verse 4 says, "For every house is built by some man, but he that built all things is God." Since Jesus created all things (John 1:3), He therefore is God.

III. JESUS IS SUPERIOR IN HIS PERSON (vv. 5-6)

"And Moses verily was faithful in all his house, as a servant, for a testimony of those things which were to be spoken after; but Christ as a son over his own house, whose house are we, if we hold fast the confidence and the rejoicing of the hope firm unto the end."

Moses was a servant, but Jesus is a Son. There's a big difference between the two. In John 8:35 Jesus says, "The servant abideth not in the house forever; but the Son abideth forever." Servants come and go, but sons are sons for life.

A. The Servant

Verse 5 tells us that Moses was a faithful servant. "Servant" (Gk., *therapōn*) denotes a dignified position. Moses was a faithful, obedient servant, a good steward of God's household. There are eight references to Moses' obedience in Exodus 40, whereas Exodus 35-40 contains twenty-two. As exalted as Moses was, however, Jesus was more exalted. Note that God compares Jesus with the best of men, and He still is infinitely greater. Were He compared with the worst of men, that would be nothing. But He was greater than the greatest of men.

18

B. The Shadow

We learn from verse 5 that Moses' faithfulness was a testimony to greater things that were yet to come in Christ. Hebrews 10:1 says, "The law, having a shadow of good things to come and not the very image of the things, can never with those sacrifices which they offered year by year continually make those who come to it perfect." The law was the shadow of good things yet to come in Christ. Jesus said, "Had ye believed Moses, ye would have believed me; for he wrote of me" (John 5:46). It is impossible to truly believe what Moses wrote yet reject Jesus.

Luke 24:27 says of Jesus that "beginning at Moses and all the prophets, he expounded unto them [two disciples on the road to Emmaus], in all the scriptures, the things concerning himself." Jesus explained what the Old Testament said about Him.

Paul also used Moses' writings to teach about Jesus. In Acts 28:23 we find that "when they had appointed him a day, there came many to him into his lodging, to whom he expounded and testified the kingdom of God, persuading them concerning Jesus, both out of the law of Moses, and out of the prophets, from morning till evening." That means there was a lot about Jesus in Moses' writings. So Hebrews 3:5 tells us that Moses was only a servant who pointed to something that would come later.

C. The Son

Unlike Moses, Christ was not a servant in another man's house but a Son over His own house. Christ's house is the church. In 1 Timothy 3:15 Paul writes, "But if I tarry long, that thou mayest know how thou oughtest to behave thyself in the house of God, which is the church of the living God." Believers are God's house.

D. The Security

1. The problem

How can we be sure that we're really of His house? Hebrews 3:6 gives the answer: "If we hold fast the confidence and the rejoicing of the hope firm unto the end." Some people have misunderstood that verse—they have thought it is saying we must keep ourselves saved, that we could lose our salvation. But since we couldn't save ourselves to begin with, how could we keep ourselves saved? What this verse is saying is that perseverance is proof of salvation. Those who are truly part of the house of God will not depart from the faith. Whoever leaves proves he never belonged in the first place (1 John 2:19). That truth is repeatedly emphasized in Hebrews because the Jews the writer was addressing were in danger of falling away. And those who fall away give evidence that they have never received Christ. True saints persevere.

2. The passages

   a) John 8:31

   "Then said Jesus to those Jews who believed on him, if ye continue in my word, then are ye my disciples indeed."

   The word translated "indeed" (Gk., *aléthos*) means "genuine" or "real." People often ask me about someone they know who once professed Christ but now has fallen away and repudiates God. The explanation for such people is found in this verse. By not continuing in Christ, they indicate that they never were genuine disciples. They professed faith but never possessed it.

   b) John 6:39

   "This is the Father's will who hath sent me, that of all that he hath given me I should lose nothing, but should raise it up again at the last day."

   One of the clearest truths of the New Testament is that the Lord keeps those who belong to Him. Jesus has never lost anyone from His household and never will.

c) James 1:22-25

"Be ye doers of the word and not hearers only, deceiving your own selves. For if any be a hearer of the word, and not a doer, he is like a man beholding his natural face in a mirror. For he beholdeth himself, and goeth his way, and immediately forgetteth what manner of man he was. But whosoever looketh into the perfect law of liberty, and continueth in it, he being not a forgetful hearer but a doer of the work, this man shall be blessed in his deed."

d) Colossians 1:22-23

"In the body of his flesh through death, to present you holy and unblamable and unreprovable in his sight, if ye continue in the faith."

e) 2 John 9

"Whosoever transgresseth, and abideth not in the doctrine of Christ, hath not God. He that abideth in the doctrine of Christ, he hath both the Father and the Son."

f) 1 John 2:19

"They went out from us, but they were not of us; for if they had been of us, they would no doubt have continued with us; but they went out, that they might be made manifest that they were not all of us."

g) Hebrews 10:38-39

"Now the just shall live by faith; but if any man draw back, my soul shall have no pleasure in him. But we are not of them who draw back unto perdition, but of them that believe to the saving of the soul."

Conclusion

Hebrews 3:1-6 says two important things. First, we need to examine ourselves and make sure our faith is genuine (2 Cor. 13:5). The Lord gives a sobering warning in Matthew 7:22-23: "Many will say to me in that day, Lord, Lord, have we not prophesied in thy name? And in thy name have cast out demons? And in thy name done many wonderful works? And then will I profess unto them, I never knew you; depart from me, ye that work iniquity." Second, it exhorts those of us who are Christians already to consider Jesus. We need to live our whole lives focusing on Him. He is all we need. Paul said it well when he said: "Ye are complete in Him" (Col. 2:10).

Focusing on the Facts

1. Describe the three groups of people to whom the book of Hebrews was addressed (see pp. 8-9).
2. What is the message to all three groups (see p. 9)?
3. How did the writer of Hebrews prove that the New Covenant is superior to the Old (see p. 9)?
4. The theme of the book of Hebrews may be summed up in the words _____ _____ (see p. 9).
5. What was the main reason that the Jewish people held Moses in such high regard (see p. 10)?
6. Does the writer's use of "brethren" indicate that the entire book of Hebrews was written to believers? Why or why not (see pp. 11-12)?
7. Since believers already know Christ, why does the writer of Hebrews tell us to consider Him (see p. 13)?
8. What was Paul's most important exhortation to Timothy in 2 Timothy 2 (see p. 14)?
9. What are two characteristics of an ambassador (see p. 15)?
10. What quality did Jesus and Moses have in common (see pp. 16-17)?
11. The household of God in the Old Testament consisted of _____ and _____ _____ (see p. 17).
12. What is Christ's household? Support your answer from Scripture (see p. 17).
13. How does Hebrews 3:4 support Christ's deity (see p. 18)?

14. Jesus is greater than Moses because He is a _____ while Moses was a _____ (see p. 18).
15. Name three verses that show Moses wrote about Christ (see p. 19).
16. Does Hebrews 3:6 teach that a Christian could lose his salvation? Explain (see pp. 19-20).
17. How would you explain someone who once professed faith in Christ but then fell away from the Christian faith (see p. 20)?
18. What are two important things we learn from Hebrews 3:1-6 (see p. 22)?

Pondering the Principles

1. The writer of Hebrews repeatedly exhorts weaker Christians who were enmeshed in legalism to rest in the sufficiency of Christ. Is legalism a problem for you? Do you feel God likes you when you perform well and dislikes you when you don't? Do you equate spirituality with mere knowledge of Bible facts, holding an office in the church, or not doing certain things, such as drinking, dancing, smoking, or listening to rock music? One of the best antidotes for legalism is to understand that we are accepted by God because of our position in Christ, not because of our works. If you struggle with legalism, study the following Scripture verses carefully: Romans 5:1; 8:1; Galatians 3:3; 5:1; Ephesians 1:3, 7; Colossians 2:10; 1 John 4:9-10; Jude 24. You may want to memorize them and recall them to mind when you are tempted to think your acceptance by God is based on your performance.

2. Moses is commended in this passage for his faithfulness as a steward of what God gave him. Could it be said of you that you are a faithful steward? How well are you managing the resources God has entrusted to you, such as your time, money, spiritual gifts, children, or ministry? Are you holding back any of those areas and not acknowledging God's rightful ownership? Remember, a steward doesn't own anything; he merely manages it for the owner. Ask God to help you to be a faithful steward of all He has given you and to show you if you are being unfaithful in managing any of His resources.

3. Are you running the Christian race with your eyes on Jesus, or have you become distracted by the things of this world? Go somewhere where you can be alone and take a hard look at your priorities. Do they show that you are laying up treasure in heaven or treasure on earth? Are the eternal realities of God's Word, God's people, and God's kingdom at the top of your priority list or closer to the bottom? Ask God to show you how your priorities need to change, and then take practical steps to change them. Finally, make yourself accountable to some other believers to act on those changes.

4. The apostle Paul expresses a deep desire to know Christ better in Philippians 3:10. How well do you know Christ? If it has been some time since you have studied the life of Christ, why not do that? A good way to begin is to purchase a harmony of the gospels and use it as the basis of your study. In addition, there are a number of good books available on the life and ministry of Jesus (your pastor or local Christian bookstore can recommend some). As you study, ask God to reveal to you the majesty and glory of His Son.

2
Harden Not Your Hearts

Outline

Introduction

Lesson

Introduction

From Genesis to Revelation, the Bible warns that the wrath of God
is inevitable if men continue in sin. Since God takes no pleasure in

the death of the wicked (Ezek. 18:32), is not willing that any should perish, and wants all to come to repentance (2 Pet. 3:9), He continuously warns men. Hebrews 3:7-19 is one such warning. God warns unredeemed men to turn to Jesus Christ before it's too late.

Many people believe the facts of the gospel but have never committed themselves to Jesus Christ. To know the truth but not act on it brings upon a man a worse judgment than not knowing it. Hebrews 3:7-19 is a warning to men who know the gospel but because of love of sin or fear of persecution have not committed themselves to what they know is true.

Don't Get Burned!

Imagine you're on the tenth floor of a burning hotel. The firemen below are holding a net and yelling for you to jump. You look out the window and wonder whether you should trust yourself to those firemen. The fire is spreading rapidly, and you don't have much time. But rather than commit yourself and jump, you're concerned about your possessions. You grab your belongings and try to escape down the stairs. You don't make it, however, and are consumed by flames. Hebrews 3:7-19 is the Holy Spirit's way of saying, "Jump!" There is no escape from the fires of God's wrath except through a total commitment to Jesus Christ.

The Jewish people addressed in this passage had heard the gospel directly from the apostles and prophets. They were in danger of becoming what the Bible calls apostates—those who know the truth but willfully reject it. To get his warning across, the author used an illustration from the Old Testament. Since the writer had just talked about Moses (vv. 1-6), he used an illustration from the experience of Moses.

Lesson

I. THE ILLUSTRATION (vv. 7-11)

"Wherefore, as the Holy Spirit saith, Today if ye will hear his voice, harden not your hearts, as in the provocation, in the day of trial in the wilderness, when your fathers put me to the test,

26

proved me, and saw my works forty years. Wherefore, I was grieved with that generation, and said, They do always err in their heart, and they have not known my ways. So I swore in my wrath, They shall not enter into my rest."

Verses 7-11 are a quote from Psalm 95:7-11. Psalm 95 refers to Israel's disobedience and rejection of Moses while in the wilderness. After four hundred years in Egypt, Israel was led out through a series of plagues culminating in the death of all the first-born of Egypt. God also performed miracles for Israel in the wilderness, including the parting of the Red Sea. In spite of those miracles, the people still failed to believe God. That's a classic illustration of unbelief in the face of overwhelming evidence. As a result, God judged them, and they wandered for nearly forty years in the wilderness until all that generation died. Just as the psalmist used that as a warning to the people of his day, so the writer of Hebrews warns his readers not to do what the people of Moses' day did.

Who Really Wrote the Bible?

Verse 7 says the Holy Spirit was the author of Psalm 95. Inspiration is the Holy Spirit's speaking through the minds of God's human instruments. When you read a verse in your Bible, you are reading the words of the Spirit of God, the author of Scripture. Second Peter 1:21 says, "Prophecy came not at any time by the will of man, but holy men of God spoke as they were moved by the Holy Spirit." The Holy Spirit inspired every word of the original autographs of Scripture. That's why it is such a serious matter to deny the inerrancy of the Bible.

A. The Plea

1. The meaning of "today"

This word is used frequently in this section (3:7, 13, 15; 4:7). It doesn't necessarily signify a twenty-four-hour period but rather indicates urgency. The writer of Hebrews urges those who know the truth of the gospel not to harden their hearts as Israel did. The apostle Paul echoes that thought in 2 Corinthians 6:2: "Behold now is the accepted time; behold, now is the day of salvation."

D. L. Moody was preaching in Chicago on October 8, 1871. A biographer writes, "Before him was the largest congregation he had ever addressed in the city. He concluded with a blunder that he had called the biggest in his life, one which he vowed he would give his right hand to recall. He, D. L. Moody, gave them a week to decide for Christ" (Richard K. Curtis, *They Called Him Mister Moody* [Grand Rapids: Eerdmans, 1962], p. 150). That night the great Chicago fire broke out, and many of the people who had heard him speak were killed. Moody said that was the last time he ever told anyone to postpone a decision for Christ.

The Bible teaches the urgency of immediately responding to the gospel—you may not have another opportunity. "Today" signifies the present time of grace while God's blessings are still available. People today need to heed the warning of the writer of Hebrews not to put off a decision regarding salvation.

2. The menace of a hard heart

Verse 7 also says, "If ye will hear his voice." Hearing God is a matter of your own will, and there is always a danger of hardening your heart as Israel did. Paul said it is possible for one's conscience to become seared, as with a hot iron (1 Tim. 4:2). The Greek word translated "seared" means "burned," and when skin is severely burned and scar tissue forms, it becomes insensitive. When I was in college, I was thrown out of a car going about seventy-five miles an hour, and I slid about one hundred yards on my back. As a result, I had third-degree burns over sixty-four square inches on my back, and the scar tissue that has resulted is insensitive—it's been seared.

There is a danger that someone who hears the gospel repeatedly but rejects it will develop a seared conscience and no longer be sensitive to what God is saying to him. That is why the writer of Hebrews urges his readers to respond today to the gospel and not harden their hearts. The time to respond to Jesus Christ is when your heart is soft and your conscience is convicted, lest you end up with the kind of hard heart of which Proverbs 29:1 warns.

B. The Pictures

1. Israel at Meribah

The "provocation in the day of trial in the wilderness" (v. 8) refers back to an incident described in Exodus 17:1-7: "All the congregation of the children of Israel journeyed from the wilderness of Sin, after their journeys, according to the commandment of the Lord, and encamped in Rephidim: and there was no water for the people to drink. Wherefore the people did strive with Moses, and said, Give us water that we may drink. And Moses said unto them, Why strive ye with me? Wherefore do ye put the Lord to the test? And the people thirsted there for water; and the people murmured against Moses, and said, Why hast thou brought us up out of Egypt, to kill us and our children and our cattle with thirst? And Moses cried unto the Lord, saying, What shall I do unto this people? They are almost ready to stone me. And the Lord said unto Moses, Go on before the people, and take with thee of the elders of Israel; and thy rod, wherewith thou smotest the river, take in thy hand, and go. Behold, I will stand before thee there upon the rock in Horeb; and thou shalt smite the rock, and there shall come water out of it, that the people may drink. And Moses did so in the sight of the elders of Israel. And he called the name of the place Massah [which means trial or tested], and Meribah [which means striving], because of the striving of the children of Israel, and because they tested the Lord, saying, Is the Lord among us or not?"

Although God had just delivered Israel from bondage in Egypt through a series of miracles, parted the Red Sea to allow them to escape the pursuing Egyptian army, and given them manna to eat, they still doubted whether God was among them. That's the character of unbelief—it never has enough proof. People who have had their questions answered but keep on demanding more proof give evidence that they are unwilling to act on what they know to be true.

The writer of Hebrews warns his readers not to harden their hearts as the people of Israel did when they got thirsty at Meribah and Massah. It is a serious matter to put God to the test. Jesus rebuked Satan with the words "Thou shalt not put the Lord, thy God, to the test" (Matt. 4:7). Despite the overwhelming evidence, Israel failed to believe God's promise; they would not take the step of committing themselves in faith to God.

2. Israel at Kadesh-barnea

According to Hebrews 3:9, Israel kept putting God to the test for forty years, not just at Meribah but all through the wilderness. Numbers 14 tells us how it all began. Israel was camped at Kadesh-barnea, and spies were sent ahead into the land of Canaan to spy out the land. When the spies returned and reported the strength of the inhabitants of the land, the Israelites failed once again to believe God. As a result, God declared that none of the men of that generation (except Caleb and Joshua, who had believed) would enter the Promised Land: "All those men who have seen my glory, and my miracles, which I did in Egypt and in the wilderness, and have put me to the test now these ten times, and have not hearkened to my voice; Surely they shall not see the land which I swore to give unto the fathers, neither shall any of them that provoked me see it" (vv. 22-23). God had given the Israelites evidence of His ability to lead them into Canaan, and since they refused to believe Him, He did not allow them to enter the Promised Land.

The unbelief of Israel stands as a warning for all men. Just as Israel had sufficient evidence of God's faithfulness in their day, so we have sufficient evidence that Jesus Christ is Lord, the Savior of mankind. He died on a cross for our sins and rose again three days later. Unbelief in the face of such overwhelming evidence is tragic indeed.

3. Israel in the wilderness

Hebrews 3:10 continues the account of Israel in the wilderness: "Wherefore, I was grieved with that generation, and said, They do always err in their heart, and they have not known my ways." The Greek word translated "grieved" means more than just unhappy. It means God was aggravated, vexed, displeased, or angered. The Israelites thought they could go their own way and do their own thing, but they couldn't. Sin is deceiving—it makes darkness seem light, bitter seem sweet, bondage seem liberty, and wrong seem right.

"They" in verse 10 is an inclusive term—it refers to the entire generation that died in the wilderness. It was totally and habitually evil. That's why I don't think Hebrews 3:7-11 refers to believers who are "out of fellowship." People who constantly, habitually follow evil are unbelievers. Deuteronomy 9:7 describes the Israelites as having been rebellious against the Lord from the day they left Egypt.

The illustration closes with a powerful statement in verse 11: "So I swore in my wrath, they shall not enter into my rest." That is a reference to Canaan, the Promised Land. It implies resting from wandering and toil. Because the Israelites sinned and continued in unbelief, God decreed that that whole generation would die and only their children (who had not rebelled) would go into the land. Note that verse 11 says that God swore an oath. When God makes an oath to Himself, it's a binding oath. The wilderness generation had reached the limit of God's patience.

Even the generation that did enter Canaan failed to fully enter God's rest. God told them to destroy the Canaanites, who were an especially vile people. The Canaanites were so evil that they buried live babies in jars in the walls of buildings they built. God wanted them destroyed and was planning to use Israel as His instrument of judgment. But instead Israel moved in with them and consequently never knew the rest God had planned for them. The fate of the wilderness generation

31

is a graphic illustration of how God treats those who know the truth but harden their hearts.

II. THE INVITATION (v. 12)

"Take heed, brethren, lest there be in any of you an evil heart of unbelief, in departing from the living God."

On the basis of the illustration in verses 7-11, the writer of Hebrews invites his readers to respond to the truth and not fall away. "Brethren" is not a reference to Christians; when the writer addresses Christians, he refers to them as "holy brethren" (e.g., 3:1). Verse 12 is addressed to fellow Jews. He warns them that if they reject Christianity they are departing from God.

A. The Depravity of Unbelief

The greatest evil in the world is unbelief. It is the worst sin you can commit because it keeps you from salvation. The non-Christians addressed in Hebrews were on the verge of faith and may even have claimed to be Christians. They would never have admitted to being openly against Christ, but they were. No matter how close you are to faith in Jesus Christ, if you never commit yourself to Him, you have an evil heart of unbelief. Your punishment will be all the more severe because you have departed from what you knew to be the truth. Hebrews 6:6 says of such people, "It is impossible to renew them again to repentance" (NASB). When a person hears the truth of Jesus Christ, acknowledges that it is true, and then turns his back and walks away, there is nothing more God can do.

B. The Departure of Unbelievers

"Departing" (Gk., *aphistēmi*) means "to stand afar off from" or "to stand apart from." Those who depart wind up standing apart from God as doomed apostates. Note also that verse 12 refers to God as "the living God." To reject Jesus Christ is not to reject a form of religion or a creed; it's to walk away from the living God.

III. THE INSTRUCTION (vv. 13-18)

"But exhort one another daily, while it is called Today, lest any of you be hardened through the deceitfulness of sin. For we are made partakers of Christ, if we hold the beginning of our confidence steadfast unto the end, while it is said, Today if ye will hear his voice, harden not your hearts, as in the provocation. For who, when they had heard, did provoke? Did not all that came out of Egypt by Moses? But with whom was he grieved forty years? Was it not with them that had sinned, whose carcasses fell in the wilderness? And to whom swore he that they should not enter into his rest, but to them that believed not?"

"Exhort" (Gk., *parakaleō*) refers to one called alongside to help. The noun form of this verb is a name given to the Holy Spirit (John 14:16). The writer exhorts his readers to get alongside each other and urge one another to turn to Christ. I'm not ashamed to beg people to come to Jesus Christ. The apostle Paul said, "We beg you in Christ's stead, be ye reconciled to God" (2 Cor. 5:20).

"Deceitfulness" refers to trickery or stratagem. Sin is tricky—it frequently masks itself. Men may become hardened by it without even realizing it. They hear the gospel of Jesus Christ time and time again but don't respond.

A. The Decision of Men

Hebrews 10:38-39 gives us the decision all men must face: "The just shall live by faith; but if any man draw back, my soul shall have no pleasure in him. But we are not of them who draw back unto perdition, but of them that believe to the saving of the soul." Either you believe and are saved or you are damned. Sin would try to deceive us into thinking that falling back isn't that bad, or that the price is too high to be a Christian. It would try to tell us that we're self-sufficient and can make it on our own.

1. Those who make the right choice

Verse 14 gives us the mark of those whose faith is genuine: "We are made partakers of Christ, if we hold the beginning of our confidence steadfast unto the end." The greatest proof that someone is a believer is his continuation in the faith. People sometimes ask me about someone they know who used to attend church, claiming to be a Christian, but now has fallen away from the faith. My reply is the fact he left proves he was never saved. The true branch in John 15 remains attached to the vine. Hebrews 3:14 repeats the thought of verse 6, which says we are of the house of Christ if we remain confident to the end.

2. Those who make the wrong choice

First John 2:19 says in reference to those who depart from the faith, "They went out from us, but they were not of us; for if they had been of us, they would no doubt have continued with us; but they went out, that they might be made manifest that they were not all of us." I've met too many people who made an initial commitment to Christ that turned out not to be real. They're never at prayer time, they've no desire to witness or read Scripture, and they never talk about the things of God. They lead a worldly life-style, yet they claim to be Christians. Despite their claim, they give evidence that they never were real. Jesus says of them in Matthew 7:22-23, "Many will say to me in that day, Lord, Lord, have we not prophesied in thy name? And in thy name have cast out demons? And in thy name done many wonderful works? And then I will profess unto them, I never knew you; depart from me, ye that work iniquity."

B. The Decision of God

In verse 15 the writer repeats for emphasis the injunction of verses 7-8. He then goes on to add in verses 16-17, "Who, when they had heard, did provoke? Did not all that came out of Egypt by Moses? But with whom was he grieved forty years? Was it not with them that had sinned, whose carcasses fell in the wilderness?" God was angry with the whole generation of unbelieving people and sentenced them to wander until they died, never entering into His rest. Verse 18 says, "To whom sware he that they should not enter into his rest, but to them that believed not?" The principle is clear: unbelief brings about tragic consequences.

IV. THE ISSUE (v. 19)

"So we see that they could not enter in because of unbelief."

Verse 19 is the crux of the passage. Those who fall short of salvation do so because of unbelief. God's blessings are available to those who take hold of them by faith. Some people claim they can't live by faith—they have a pragmatic, empirical mind that has to have all the facts. However, everyone lives by faith. You live by faith when you eat in a restaurant. You live by faith when you drive. No one drives in constant fear that around the next bend he will smash into a forty-foot-high concrete wall; we trust the people who made the highways. When crossing a bridge, we don't expect it to end half-way out. If you can put your faith in the highway department and the people who prepare your food, you can certainly put your faith in the God of the universe. You'll never enter God's rest unless you commit your life to Christ. Continuing in unbelief will inevitably bring the judgment of God.

A. The Warning of Jude

Jude said, "I will, therefore, put you in remembrance, though ye once knew this, that the Lord, having saved the people out of the land of Egypt, afterward destroyed them that believed not" (Jude 5).

B. The Warning of the Author of Hebrews

Hebrews 12:25 says, "See that ye refuse not him that speaketh. For if they escaped not who refused him that spoke on earth, much more shall not we escape, if we turn away from him that speaketh from heaven." Moses was the one who spoke on earth, while Jesus was the One who spoke from heaven. If those who refused to listen to Moses failed to escape judgment, how will those who refuse to hear Jesus escape?

C. The Warning of Solomon

Solomon gave this warning in Proverbs 29:1: "He that, being oft reproved, hardeneth his neck, shall suddenly be destroyed, and that without remedy." To harden yourself against God is to bring unavoidable judgment upon yourself. I urge you to heed the words of the Holy Spirit in Hebrews 3:7-19 and not harden your heart.

Focusing on the Facts

1. Why does God warn men (see pp. 25-26)?
2. True or false: Those who know the truth of the gospel and reject it will be judged more severely than those who have never heard (see p. 26).
3. What are two reasons some people don't commit themselves to what they know is true (see p. 26)?
4. What is an apostate (see p. 26)?
5. Why does the writer of Hebrews quote from Psalm 95 (see p. 27)?
6. In your own words, how would you define inspiration (see p. 27)?
7. What could ultimately happen to someone who continues to reject the gospel (see p. 28)?
8. Why was God angry with the wilderness generation (see p. 31)?
9. True or false: The generation that entered Canaan—in contrast to those who died in the wilderness—fully entered God's rest (see p. 31).
10. Is verse 12 addressed to Christians or non-Christians? Defend your answer (see p. 32).
11. What is the worst sin you could commit (see p. 32)?
12. What is the greatest proof that someone is a Christian (see p. 34)?
13. How could you respond to someone who said he couldn't live by faith (see p. 35)?

Pondering the Principles

1. Israel's experiences in the wilderness are an example of behavior to avoid. The Bible has much to say about the power of example. It warns us against following bad examples (Lev. 18:2-3; Eph. 4:17) and encourages us to follow good examples (Heb. 12:2-3; James 5:10). What kind of examples are you following? Are you patterning your life after worldly people or godly people? What kind of example are you setting for your spouse, your children, your friends, your fellow employees, and other believers? Can you say with Paul, "Be imitators of me, just as I also am of Christ" (1 Cor. 11:1, NASB)? Begin today "in speech, conduct, love, faith and purity [to] show yourself an example of those who believe" (1 Tim. 4:12, NASB).

2. Do you know someone who professes to be a Christian but has walked away from God? On the basis of what you've learned in this chapter, how would you evaluate him? Begin to pray for him, and ask God to give you an opportunity to share with him the warning of Hebrews 3:7-19 and the boldness to confront him with the consequences if he continues to forsake the faith.

3. Despite all that God had done for the Israelites in miraculously delivering them from bondage in Egypt and in sustaining them in the wilderness, they still grumbled against Him at Meribah. Do you find yourself concentrating on what God has done for you (being thankful) or on what He hasn't done for you (becoming a grumbler)? If you struggle with being a grumbler, memorize 1 Thessalonians 5:18 and Philippians 2:14.

3
Entering God's Rest

Outline

Introduction
A. The Availability of Rest
B. The Definitions of Rest
    1. To cease from action
    2. To be free from worry
    3. To be settled
    4. To be secure
    5. To have something to lean on

Lesson
I. The Availability of Rest (v. 1)
    A. The Forfeiture of Rest
    B. The Promise of Rest
        1. To Israel
        2. To the church
            a) By exercising faith in Christ
            b) By acknowledging our sin to God
II. The Basis of Rest (vv. 2-7)
    A. Personal Faith (vv. 2-5)
        1. The necessity of faith
            a) The faith that doesn't save
            b) The faith that does save
                (1) 1 Thessalonians 2:13
                (2) 2 Thessalonians 2:13
                (3) James 1:22
        2. The cruciality of faith
        3. The rest of faith
            a) Rest defined
            b) Rest forfeited
            c) Rest recovered

Introduction

Chapter four continues the warning to unbelievers that began in Hebrews 3:7. Throughout this section, the writer of Hebrews illustrates his point with the nation of Israel. The Israelites left Egypt but were stopped short of the Promised Land by their failure to believe God. An entire generation never entered the full rest of Canaan. The warning is not to do what Israel did but to enter God's rest through faith in Jesus Christ.

A. The Availability of Rest

The rest of Canaan pictures the spiritual rest that comes by faith in Christ. God has a rest that is far greater than Canaan—eternal rest available by faith in Christ.

B. The Definitions of Rest

The dictionary gives the following definitions of *rest*:

1. To cease from action

The word *rest* means to cease from labor or exertion. Applying that to God's rest, it means no more self-effort—no more trying to please God by your fleshly works. Rest involves cessation from legalistic activity; we rest in free grace.

2. To be free from worry

Some people are never at peace because they're always bothered about something. To rest means to be free from whatever disturbs you or causes you to worry. It means in this sense to be quiet, still, peaceful, and free from guilt. To enter God's rest means to be at peace with God—to possess the perfect peace that God gives. It means to be free from guilt, because our sin is forgiven.

3. To be settled

God's rest is the type of rest in which a man is established in Christ and does not run from philosophy to philosophy. He is no longer blown about by every wind of doctrine but is rooted and grounded in the truth of Christ.

4. To be secure

To enter God's rest is to be secure, having absolute trust and confidence in God's care for you.

5. To have something to lean on

To enter God's rest means that you can lean on Him. You can rely on God for support, trusting Him to supply all your needs.

There are two final definitions of rest not found in a dictionary. The Bible speaks of rest in the millennial kingdom and rest for eternity in heaven. That's what God is promising, and that's what He calls rest. Many people fail to believe in God's promises and thus do not enter into rest because of their unbelief.

Lesson

I. THE AVAILABILITY OF REST (v. 1)

"Let us, therefore, fear lest, a promise being left us of entering into his rest, any of you should seem to come short of it."

A. The Forfeiture of Rest

"Therefore" takes us back to what the writer has said previously about Israel. The unbelieving, fence-sitting Jews whom the writer is addressing had reason to fear after being reminded of Israel's forfeiture of rest. Unbelief brings about fearful consequences.

Scripture indicates that Christians don't need to fear. Jesus said, "Let not your heart be troubled, neither let it be afraid" (John 14:27). Paul told Timothy that "God hath not given us the spirit of fear" (2 Tim. 1:7). However, unbelievers have reason to fear. It's not a trifling thing to fool with the rest that God offers, "for our God is a consuming fire" (Heb. 12:29).

B. The Promise of Rest

1. To Israel

Verse 1 says, "A promise being left for us." The "us" is a reference to the Jewish people. What the writer of Hebrews wants to make clear is that when Israel fell because of unbelief, that didn't mean the end of God's rest for them. When Israel failed in the wilderness, God didn't forsake them and start over with another people.

Is God Finished with Israel?

Many Jewish people who had heard the gospel were fearful that Israel had forfeited any possibility of entering God's rest because of what they had done to their Messiah. Many people today teach that when Israel rejected Jesus, they forfeited their right to God's blessing. They believe God is no longer dealing with Israel but only with the church. Therefore they conclude there will be no restoration of Israel and no kingdom for Israel. That position is known as amillennialism and is widely held today. However, Hebrews 4:1 says that the promise has not been removed from Israel.

One of the great passages in the Bible that indicates God is not finished with Israel is in Acts 3. Peter is preaching and says in verses 14-15, "Ye denied the Holy One and the Just, and desired a murderer to be granted unto you; and killed the Prince of life." It seems from those verses that Israel must have forfeited everything. However in verses 25-26 Peter goes on to say, "Ye are the sons of the prophets, and of the covenant which God made with our fathers, saying unto Abraham, And in thy seed shall all the kindreds of the earth be blessed. Unto you first God, having raised up His Son, Jesus, sent him to bless you, in turning away every one of you from his iniquities." Even though the Jewish people had killed their Messiah, they were still heirs of the unconditional covenant that God made with Abraham. Following the resurrection of Christ and the birth of the church, the Jewish people were the first to be evangelized. God did not write off Israel. Paul says in Romans 11:1, "Hath God cast away his people [Israel]? God forbid." And so the writer of Hebrews affirms there is a promise left to Israel. Rest is still available.

The phrase "any of you should seem to come short of it" at the end of Hebrews 4:1 could be more accurately translated "lest you think you have come too late to enter into the rest of God." The author is telling his Jewish audience not to think it's too late to enter God's rest.

2. To the church

   a) By exercising faith in Christ

      There is a perfect rest available to us through faith in Christ. In Matthew 7:26-27 Jesus says, "Every one that heareth these sayings of mine, and doeth them not, shall be likened unto a foolish man, who built his house upon the sand. And the rain descended, and the floods came, and the winds blew and beat upon that house, and it fell; and great was the fall of it." Jesus warns against missing grace by failing to exercise faith in Him.

   b) By acknowledging our sin to God

      Some people fear they are too great sinners to be forgiven, but that's not true. People who acknowledge their sin are the kind of people God likes to deal with. Paul says of himself in 1 Timothy 1:15, "This is a faithful saying, and worthy of all acceptance, that Christ Jesus came into the world to save sinners, of whom I am chief." You may be too much of a sinner to deserve salvation—no one deserves salvation—but you're not too much of a sinner for the grace of God to handle (Rom. 5:6-8, 20; Matt. 9:12-13).

The Littlest Awful Sinner

My dad told me about a five-year-old boy who came into a prayer room after church service and said, "I want to receive Christ." The counselors told him he could pray and ask Jesus into his heart, and this is how he began his prayer: "God, I don't know if You can save an awful sinner like me, but if You can I want You to." God can save even an awful sinner like that! You're never too far gone for God to deal with you. If your heart is tender and you're sensitive to what the Spirit of God is saying, now is the time to listen to His call. God's rest is still available.

II. THE BASIS OF REST (vv. 2-7)

A. Personal Faith (vv. 2-5)

"For unto us was the gospel preached, as well as unto them; but the word preached did not profit them, not being mixed with faith in them that heard it. For we who have believed do enter into rest, as he said, As I have sworn in my wrath, if they shall enter into my rest; although the works were finished from the foundation of the world. For he spoke in a certain place of the seventh day in this way, And God did rest the seventh day from all his works. And in this place again, If they shall enter into my rest."

"Gospel" (v. 2) should be translated "good news." That word has a specific connotation in the New Testament, but it here refers to the good news about rest preached in the Old Testament.

1. The necessity of faith

Although the good news about God's rest was preached to Israel, it did them no good because they failed to believe it. Some people have the mistaken idea that they can become Christians through osmosis just by being in the church. However, hearing the gospel doesn't mean anything unless you believe it with your whole heart. It's tragic to realize that hell is going to be populated with people who will say to Jesus, "Lord, Lord, have we not prophesied in thy name? And in thy name have cast out demons? And in thy name done many wonderful works?" only to hear Him reply, "I never knew you; depart from me, ye that work iniquity" (Matt. 7:22-23).

a) The faith that doesn't save

This was an important message for the author's audience to hear. They thought they were safe because they had the law as a heritage. Paul says to such people in Romans 2:25, "Circumcision verily profiteth, if thou keep the law; but if thou be a breaker of the law, thy circumcision is made uncircumcision." Circumcision, Paul says, is meaningless unless you keep the law.

If a police officer stops you for speeding, you could have the entire Vehicle Code memorized and it wouldn't help you—you'd still get the ticket. Merely having the necessary information does not help unless you act on it; in fact, it makes you all the more responsible. Unless the information you have is mixed with faith, it profits you nothing.

b) The faith that does save

(1) 1 Thessalonians 2:13

"For this cause also thank we God without ceasing because, when ye received the word of God which ye heard of us, ye received it, not as the word of men but as it is in truth, the word of God, which effectually worketh also in you that believe."

(2) 2 Thessalonians 2:13

"We are bound to give thanks always to God for you, brethren beloved of the Lord, because God

45

hath from the beginning chosen you to salvation through sanctification of the Spirit and belief of the truth."

(3) James 1:22

"Be ye doers of the word and not hearers only, deceiving your own selves."

2. The cruciality of faith

Hebrews 4:3 tells us the destiny of those who exercise faith and those who don't. The first part of the verse says, "We who have believed do enter into rest." Note it doesn't say we are on the way to rest; it states we are in it. Every Christian is in God's rest. That is just another way of saying we are saved.

God says of those who fail to exercise faith, "As I have sworn in my wrath, if they shall enter into my rest." A better translation of that last phrase is, "They shall not enter into my rest." That expresses God's attitude toward those who do not exercise faith. To fail to believe the truth is to forfeit God's rest for all eternity.

3. The rest of faith

a) Rest defined

In verse 3 God defines the rest as "my rest." God's rest is not a rest of weariness or inactivity but of finished work. God's rest began after the sixth day of creation. After creating the universe, the earth, and all life (including man) in six literal days, God rested. His rest is described in verses 3-4: "Although the works were finished from the foundation of the world. For he spoke in a certain place of the seventh day in this way, And God did rest the seventh day from all his works" (cf. Gen. 2:1-2).

b) Rest forfeited

There was only one condition for Adam and Eve to remain in God's rest: believe God. However, they chose to believe Satan's lies instead and by their unbelief forfeited rest.

c) Rest recovered

The rest of the Bible records God's efforts to get man back into His rest. To do that, He had to deal with man's sin. The coming of Jesus Christ took care of the sin issue, and through the death of Christ, men may enter back into God's rest. Christ bore the sins of those who lived prior to the cross as well as those of us who live after the cross.

Verse 5 reiterates the statement of verse 3 that the unbelieving Israelites failed to enter God's rest. I believe that the people who sinned in the wilderness not only forfeited Canaan, but also forfeited the eternal life Canaan symbolized unless they exercised personal faith in God.

B. Divine Decree (v. 6)

"Seeing, therefore, it remaineth that some must enter into it, and they to whom it was first preached entered not in because of unbelief."

The second basis of rest is divine or sovereign decree. We are saved not only by our personal faith but also by God's sovereign choice before the foundation of the world (Eph. 1:4). Jesus puts both elements of salvation together in John 6 when He says, "No man can come to me, except the Father, who hath sent me, draw him" (v. 44), and "him that cometh to me I will in no wise cast out" (v. 37). How those two doctrines can be harmonized is beyond our limited ability to understand.

Hebrews 4:6 gives us the balance of what the writer said previously in this passage regarding personal faith. By God's sovereign decree, rest still remains. God does not design things for no purpose. Since He designed that there be a rest, He has always preserved a remnant throughout history to enjoy it. Although the way is narrow and few find it (Matt. 7:14), some do. Paul writes of Israel in Romans 11:5, "At this present time also there is a remnant according to the election of grace." God has selected a remnant to enter His rest, and they enter it by personal faith.

C. Immediate Action (v. 7)

"Again, he limiteth a certain day, saying in David, Today, after so long a time, as it is said, Today if ye will hear his voice, harden not your hearts."

The age of grace will not last forever. That's why the apostle Paul said, "Now is the day of salvation" (2 Cor. 6:2). Right now is God's today. In Genesis 6:3 God says, "My Spirit shall not always strive with man, for that he also is flesh: yet his days shall be an hundred and twenty years." There is a limit to His patience. The pre-Flood civilization is an example of that.

"Today" refers to the day salvation is offered. The Spirit of God urges immediate action in verse 7 because today doesn't last forever. This is the day that rest is available. Don't delay and risk missing God's rest.

III. THE NATURE OF REST (vv. 8-10)

"If Joshua had given them rest, then would he not afterward have spoken of another day. There remaineth, therefore, a rest to the people of God. For he that is entered into his rest, he also has ceased from his own works, as God did from his."

A. It Is Spiritual

The rest spoken of in this passage is not the physical rest of Canaan. Verse 8 says that Joshua failed to give Israel rest, yet he took them into Canaan. The true rest comes not through a Moses, a Joshua, or even a David; it comes through Jesus Christ. Many cults promise happiness, health, and wealth in this life, but that's never the emphasis of the Bible. Many of God's people are busy, hardworking, or even afflicted with physical suffering, yet they are in God's salvation rest.

B. It Is for Israel

The term "people of God" may refer generally to anyone who knows God, but in this passage the context reveals that it refers specifically to Israel, the people of God in the Old Testament. God's rest is promised to Israel, and I believe that He will not be finished with them until they come into His rest.

C. It Is Future

There is a final rest coming when we will cease from our work. In Revelation 14:13 John says, "I heard a voice from heaven saying unto me, Write, Blessed are the dead who die in the Lord from henceforth. Yea, saith the Spirit, that they may rest from their labors." I believe Hebrews 4:10 is a reference to that final day when we cease from our labors and enter into the presence of Jesus Christ.

IV. THE URGENCY OF REST (vv. 11-13)

"Let us labor, therefore, to enter into that rest, lest any man fall after the same example of unbelief. For the word of God is living, and powerful, and sharper than any two-edged sword, piercing even to the dividing asunder of soul and spirit, and of the joints and marrow, and is a discerner of the thoughts and intents of the heart. Neither is there any creature that is not manifest in his sight, but all things are naked and opened unto the eyes of him with whom we have to do."

The Greek word translated "labor" means "to make haste" or "to work diligently." The passage is not teaching that you can work your way to salvation but that you diligently seek to enter God's rest by faith.

A. The Power of the Word

The writer warns us to be diligent to enter into God's rest because the Word of God is living and powerful. It will pierce you to the depths of your heart to determine whether you are a genuine believer or not. Although you may claim to have faith in Jesus, if your faith is not real, the Word of God will reveal the emptiness of your profession. Several passages in Revelation illustrate the Word of God used as an instrument of judgment. In Revelation 1:16 we read, "Out of his [Jesus'] mouth went a sharp two-edged sword." In Revelation 2:16 Jesus warns the church at Pergamum to "repent, or else I will come unto thee quickly, and will fight against them with the sword of my mouth." Revelation 19:15, 21 refer to the Lord's smiting the nations with the sword of His mouth. Those passages illustrate that the Word of God is used not only in saving men but in judging them as well.

B. The Penetration of the Word

The Greek word translated "sword" (*machaira*) does not refer to a large sword but to a dagger. As a small knife that can be thrust with accuracy, God's Word penetrates to the innermost part of a man. "Discerner" is a translation of the Greek word *kritikos,* from which we get the English word *critic.* The Word of God analyzes a man's thoughts, motives, and attitudes. It penetrates all disguises and lays bare the soul.

The Greek word translated "opened" in verse 13 had two connotations in ancient times. It was used of a wrestler who seized his opponent by the throat so that he couldn't move. In such a situation, the two opponents would be face to face. The Word of God grabs us and forces us to come face to face with God. The second use of the word was in reference to the trial of a criminal. A dagger would be strapped under an accused man's chin with its point up, thus keeping him from bowing his head and forcing him to face the court. Sooner or later, all men will stand before God, whose Word will lay bare their heart and force them to face God and their own sinfulness. In light of that sobering reality, I urge you not to harden your heart.

Focusing on the Facts

1. What does the writer of Hebrews use Israel to illustrate (see p. 40)?
2. Give the dictionary and biblical definitions of the word *rest* (see pp. 40-41).
3. Why do people fail to enter God's rest (see p. 41)?

4. Does God have future plans for Israel? Support your answer with Scripture (see pp. 42-43).
5. Are there some people whose sin is too great for God to forgive? Support your answer from Scripture (see pp. 43-44).
6. Why was it not sufficient for Israel merely to know the truth (see p. 44)?
7. When did God's rest begin (see p. 46)?
8. The Bible records God's efforts to get man _____ _____ _____ (see p. 47).
9. What are the two aspects of salvation (see p. 47)?
10. What is the point of verse 7 (see p. 48)?
11. Who are the people of God referred to in verse 9 (see p. 49)?
12. The Word of God is used not only in _____ men but in _____ them as well (see p. 50).

Pondering the Principles

1. One of the blessings Christians enjoy by virtue of being in God's rest is forgiveness of sin. However, many Christians fail to experience God's forgiveness in their daily lives by struggling with feelings of guilt. If doubting God's forgiveness is a problem for you or someone you know, do a Bible study on God's forgiveness and write out your own theology of forgiveness. You may wish to use a concordance or topical Bible to help you in your research. Some of the questions you might consider are: Whom does God forgive? On what basis does He forgive? How does one obtain forgiveness? What is the extent of God's forgiveness? How does God view the person He has forgiven?

2. The rest spoken of in Hebrews 4:1-13 is a spiritual rest. God does not promise us freedom from physical suffering or hardship in this life—in fact, He warns us to expect it (Acts 14:22; 1 Thess. 3:3; 2 Tim. 3:12). If you're discouraged because being a Christian hasn't brought you health, wealth, and an easy life, meditate on Paul's instructions to Timothy in 2 Timothy 2:1-10. Ask God to give you the grace to follow His way even when it isn't the easiest.

4
Our Great High Priest

Outline

Introduction
A. The Presentation of Salvation
B. The Call to Enter Salvation
   1. Holding fast to our profession
     a) The danger of apostasy
     b) The illustration of apostasy
   2. Coming boldly to the throne of grace
     a) The invitation
     b) The inducements
       (1) Our High Priest is both God and man
       (2) Our High Priest is superior to all other high priests

Lesson
I. Christ's Perfect Priesthood (v. 14)
   A. The Position of Our High Priest
     1. He passed through the heavens
     2. He finished His work
   B. The Preeminence of Our High Priest
   C. The Perfections of Our High Priest
     1. Hebrews 7:25-26
     2. Hebrews 8:1
     3. Hebrews 9:12-14
     4. Hebrews 9:24
     5. Hebrews 10:11-12
   D. The Purpose of Our High Priest

II. Christ's Perfect Person (v. 15)
   A. Sinless Humanity
   B. Sympathetic Deity
      1. The indifferent gods of men
         a) Of the Jews
         b) Of the Greeks
      2. The caring God of the Bible
         a) His separation from sin
         b) His sympathy for sinners
III. Christ's Perfect Provision (v. 16)

Introduction

A. The Presentation of Salvation

In Hebrews 4:14-16 we have a continuation of the warning passage that began in 3:7. The writer of Hebrews has been warning his readers of the dire consequences of knowing the gospel but failing to commit themselves to Christ. Verses 14-16 present the positive basis of salvation. The writer tells his readers to enter God's rest not only because of what will happen if they don't but because of what will happen if they do. He urges them to receive Jesus Christ not only because of fear of Him but also because of His beauty; not only because of His wrath but also because of His grace; and not only because He's our judge but also because He is a merciful and faithful High Priest.

B. The Call to Enter Salvation

1. Holding fast to our profession

   a) The danger of apostasy

   The individuals the writer addresses in Hebrews 3:7–4:16 had given intellectual assent to the gospel and were on the edge of decision. He tells them to hold fast their profession in spite of the persecution they were experiencing. They were being put out of the synagogue and ostracized by their society and families. As a result, they were thinking of turning around and going back to Judaism. But that would have made them apostates, and there is no hope for such people (Heb. 6:6). Those who are truly saved will not fall away, for Hebrews 4:14 says they hold fast to their profession of faith.

b) The illustration of apostasy

Jesus illustrates the danger of apostasy in the parable of the sower in Matthew 13:19-23: "When any one heareth the word of the kingdom, and understandeth it not, then cometh the wicked one, and catcheth away that which was sown in his heart. This is he which receives seed by the wayside" (v. 19). Some people hear the gospel, but they don't dig into it to find out what it means, and Satan snatches it away. Verses 20-22 say, "He that received the seed in stony places, the same is he that heareth the word, and immediately with joy receiveth it; yet hath he not root in himself, but endureth for a while; for when tribulation or persecution ariseth because of the word, immediately he is offended. He also that received seed among the thorns is he that heareth the word; and the care of this age, and the deceitfulness of riches, choke the word, and he becometh unfruitful." Those are two more illustrations of people who made a profession of faith but then fell away.

Only the last illustration Jesus gave is of saving faith: "He that received seed in the good ground is he that heareth the word, and understandeth it, who also beareth fruit, and bringeth forth, some an hundredfold, some sixty, some thirty" (v. 23). This parable tells us why so many people who make a profession of faith end up falling away.

2. Coming boldly to the throne of grace

a) The invitation

The Greek word translated "let us come" (*proserchō-mai*) is used in several other passages in the book of Hebrews to speak of the sinner's approach to God (e.g., 7:25; 10:22; 11:6). The writer urges his readers not to fall away but to come all the way to the throne of grace, all the way up to Christ.

The Theme of the Book of Hebrews

Throughout the book of Hebrews the priesthood of Christ is exalted. Jesus is the mediator who bridges the gulf between sinful men and a holy God. Hebrews 1:3 speaks of His purging our sins. Hebrews 2:17 calls Jesus a merciful and faithful High Priest, whereas Hebrews 3:1 and 4:15 also refer to Him as our High Priest. Hebrews 7-10 expounds on the priesthood of Christ in great detail. The priesthood of Jesus Christ is the theme of the entire book of Hebrews.

---

  b) The inducements

    (1) Our High Priest is both God and man

      The task of the high priest was to represent God before the people and the people before God. Once a year the high priest would go into the Holy of Holies on the Day of Atonement and offer a sacrifice to atone for the sins of the people. A perfect high priest would know both God and men perfectly, and Jesus does. Because Jesus is the God-Man, He is the perfect High Priest who has brought God and man together.

    (2) Our High Priest is superior to all other high priests

      The book of Hebrews has already had much to say about the superiority of Christ. He is superior to the Old Testament prophets (1:1-3), angels (1:4-14), Moses (3:1-6), and Joshua (4:8). In Hebrews 4:14-16 we find that He is superior to all other high priests. Jesus has none of the weaknesses of the other priests. Because He is our High Priest, He calls men to come into God's rest. In verses 14-16, we see three features that make

Jesus our great High Priest: His perfect priesthood, His perfect person, and His perfect provision.

Lesson

I. CHRIST'S PERFECT PRIESTHOOD (v. 14)

"Seeing, then, that we have a great high priest, that is passed into the heavens, Jesus, the Son of God, let us hold fast our profession."

A. The Position of Our High Priest

1. He passed through the heavens

The correct translation of the phrase "passed into the heavens" (v. 14) is "passed through the heavens." That important phrase tells us that Jesus, following His ascension, passed through the heavens into God's presence.

2. He finished His work

On the basis of His finished work on earth, Jesus entered into God's presence. In John 17:4 Jesus says to the Father, "I have finished the work which thou gavest me to do." Paul tells us in Philippians 2:9-10 that God highly exalted Him and gave Him a name above every name, a name at which every knee should bow. The reason God so honored Jesus is that He perfectly accomplished His priestly work. Jesus performed a redemptive act that brought God and man together in an eternal relationship. That's something no human priest could ever do. Every year on Yom Kippur (the Day of Atonement) the high priest would offer a sacrifice for the sins of the people for that year. That sacrifice needed to be repeated yearly in addition to the many other sacrifices for sin that were made throughout the year. Jesus Christ, in contrast, made one sacrifice whereby He perfected forever those who are His (Heb. 10:14).

Jesus did something no other priest ever did while ministering: He sat down (Heb. 1:3). That indicates He finished His work. The high priest in Israel never sat down in the Holy of Holies—in fact, there weren't any seats, except for the Mercy Seat, and no one sat on that. When Jesus accomplished His perfect work and sat down, that indicated the work of atonement was finished. No more sacrifices needed to be made. Shortly after the book of Hebrews was written, the Temple was destroyed when the Romans sacked Jerusalem in A.D. 70. Since that time there have been no sacrifices. They are no longer needed, because Jesus made the final sacrifice.

B. The Preeminence of Our High Priest

The Old Testament priest on the Day of Atonement would take the blood of the sacrifice and go through three areas: the outer court, the Holy Place, and then through the veil into the Holy of Holies, where he would sprinkle blood on the Mercy Seat. That is described for us in Leviticus 16. Before the high priest could go in to make atonement for the sins of the people, he first had to make atonement for his own sins. He was not permitted to remain in the Holy of Holies any longer than necessary to present the blood of the sacrifice. As soon as the sacrifice was made, he left and did not return for a year.

Jesus, our great High Priest, also went through three areas: He passed through the first heaven (the earth's atmosphere), the second heaven (interstellar space), and into the third heaven (the abode of God; 2 Cor. 12:2). Unlike the high priest on the Day of Atonement, however, Jesus remains permanently in the presence of God. All sacrifices prior to Jesus were but pictures of His perfect sacrifice, which fully satisfied God. Hebrews 12:24 says, "To Jesus, the mediator of the new covenant, and to the blood of sprinkling, that speaketh better things than that of Abel." First Peter 1:2 says we're "elect according to the foreknowledge of God, the Father, through sanctification of the Spirit, unto obedience and sprinkling of the blood of Jesus Christ."

C. The Perfections of Our High Priest

The book of Hebrews exalts the perfections of Jesus, our great High Priest.

1. Hebrews 7:25-26

"He is able . . . to save them to the uttermost that come unto God by him, seeing he ever liveth to make intercession for them. For such an high priest was fitting for us, who is holy, harmless, undefiled, separate from sinners, and made higher than the heavens."

2. Hebrews 8:1

"Of the things which we have spoken this is the sum: We have such an high priest, who is seated on the right hand of the throne of the Majesty in the heavens."

3. Hebrews 9:12-14

"Neither by the blood of goats and calves, but by his own blood he entered in once into the holy place, having obtained eternal redemption for us. For if the blood of bulls and of goats, and the ashes of an heifer sprinkling the unclean, sanctifieth to the purifying of the flesh, how much more shall the blood of Christ, who through the eternal Spirit offered himself without spot to God, purge your conscience from dead works to serve the living God?"

The Bible teaches that God has designated the shedding of blood (sacrificial death) as the atonement for sin (Heb. 9:22). Jesus Christ shed His blood on our behalf that God might be satisfied. Through placing our faith in Him, His perfect sacrifice covers all our sin.

4. Hebrews 9:24

"Christ is not entered into the holy places made with hands, which are the figures of the true, but into heaven itself, now to appear in the presence of God for us."

5. Hebrews 10:11-12

   "Every priest standeth daily ministering and offering often the same sacrifices, which can never take away sins; but this man, after he had offered one sacrifice for sins forever, sat down on the right hand of God."

D. The Purpose of Our High Priest

   Jesus is now in the presence of God interceding for us. A Christian could never have any sins held against him, because Jesus is constantly interceding on our behalf. First John 1:9 says, "If we confess our sins, he is faithful and just to forgive us our sins, and to cleanse us from all unrighteousness." First John 2:1 says, "If any man sin, we have an advocate with the Father, Jesus Christ the righteous." Because of Christ's intercession Paul could say, "Who shall lay any thing to the charge of God's elect?" (Rom. 8:33). Who can accuse us of anything when Christ is interceding for us? Our Lord has accomplished what no other high priest could accomplish: He paid the penalty for our sin in full, and God is satisfied.

Do We Still Need Priests Today?

The book of Hebrews marks the end of the sacrificial system. Old Testament Judaism was based on a priesthood interceding between men and God, but when Jesus came as the final priest and offered the final sacrifice, the need for such a priesthood vanished.

There is no place in Christianity for any priesthood—that is an affront to the full and final priesthood of Jesus Christ Himself. Any priesthood on earth now implies that atonement for sin has not yet been made. Christians have no need for someone to go to God for them; Hebrews 4:16 tells us we can go directly to God's throne of grace. First Peter 2:5, 9 tells us that all Christians are priests. Every man, by faith in Jesus Christ, enters directly into God's presence. When Jesus died, the veil in the Temple was torn from top to bottom (Matt. 27:51), indicating that access to God is now forever open to those who come through His Son.

II. CHRIST'S PERFECT PERSON (v. 15)

"For we have not an high priest who cannot be touched with the feeling of our infirmities, but was in all points tempted like as we are, yet without sin."

In the phrase "Jesus, the Son of God" (v. 14) we have the messianic title of Jesus Christ. Jesus is a human name, the Greek equivalent of the Hebrew name Jehoshua or Joshua, which means "Jehovah saves." The Son of God is Christ's divine title.

A. Sinless Humanity

To many people, God seems far off and unconcerned with human affairs, but that is not true. Jesus is God the Son, but that doesn't mean He didn't experience our feelings, temptations, and suffering. Verse 15 confirms that He did. Jesus sympathizes with us. He understands. I don't want to tell my troubles to someone who doesn't understand. When I hurt, Jesus hurts. He has an unequaled capacity for sympathizing with us in every danger, trial, or situation that comes our way, because He's been through it all. He endured every form of testing that a man could endure. Some people believe Jesus can't understand how they feel because they are weak and fall into temptation, whereas Jesus successfully resisted temptation. Such people forget His agony while being tempted not to follow God's will in Gethsemane. Jesus was tempted, tested, and subjected to every kind of trial that you'll ever know.

Jesus faced a much harder battle with temptation than we do. We can experience only so much pain before we lose consciousness or go into shock. When I was thrown out of a car going about seventy-five miles an hour, I felt pain for a while, and then I didn't feel anything. There is a degree of pain we will never experience because our bodies turn off the pain before we get to that level. The same thing is true in temptation. There is a degree of temptation we never experience because we succumb long before we get to that point. Since Jesus never sinned, He experienced temptation to the uttermost extreme.

B. Sympathetic Deity

   1. The indifferent gods of men

      a) Of the Jews

         The Jewish people tended to believe that God was incapable of sharing the feelings of men. He was too distant, too far removed in nature from man to be able to identify with our feelings, temptations, and problems. Under the Old Covenant, God's dealings with His people were more indirect, more distant. Except for rare instances, even faithful believers did not experience His closeness and intimacy in the way that all believers now can.

      b) Of the Greeks

         The Stoics, whose philosophy dominated much of Greek and Roman culture in the first century, believed God's primary attribute was apathy (Gk., *apatheia*). They said in some of their writings that God is incapable of feeling joy, sorrow, gladness, grief, or any other human emotion. The Epicureans taught that the gods live in the *intermundium*, the space between the physical and spiritual worlds. They believed the gods did not participate in either world and so could hardly be expected to understand the feelings, problems, and needs of mortals, being completely detached from mankind.

   2. The caring God of the Bible

      In contrast to the uncaring gods of the Jews and Greeks, Christians have a High Priest who feels everything that men feel. That was a revolutionary concept. The God of the Bible is big enough to create the whole universe, yet He understands our hurts. We not only have a God who is there but a God who has been here as well.

      a) His separation from sin

         The Greek word translated "infirmities" (v. 15) does not refer to sin. Jesus could not relate to our sin, since

He Himself never sinned. The word refers to feebleness or weakness—all the natural limitations of humanity, including liability to sin. Jesus knew firsthand the drive of human nature toward sin. His humanity was His battleground. It is here that Jesus faced and fought sin. He was victorious but not without the most intense temptation, grief, and anguish.

The phrase at the end of verse 15, "without sin" (Gk., *choris hamartias*), indicates the complete absence of sin. Despite the constant temptation Jesus endured, He did not sin. Not the slightest taint of sin ever entered His mind. Hebrews 9:28 says, "Christ was once offered to bear the sins of many; and unto them that look for him shall he appear the second time without sin unto salvation." Jesus was just as sinless during His life on earth as He will be when He returns in glory. First John 1:5 says, "God is light, and in him is no darkness at all." Jesus had no capacity to sin because He is God. Our great High Priest sympathizes with us in our trials, yet remains without the slightest taint of sin.

b) His sympathy for sinners

Some people wonder how Jesus could understand our struggle with sin since He Himself is sinless. A surgeon may have performed hundreds of operations without ever having had surgery himself. On the other hand, a person may know nothing of surgery in spite of having had many operations himself. If you were to be operated on, which person would you choose to perform the surgery? Merely experiencing something doesn't necessarily give us an understanding of it. Jesus never sinned, yet He understands sin better than any of us. He has seen it more clearly and fought it more diligently than any of us could.

Hebrews 12:3-4 says, "Consider him [Jesus] that endured such contradiction of sinners against himself, lest ye be wearied and faint in your minds. Ye have not yet resisted unto blood, striving against sin." If you want to talk to someone who understands the power of sin, talk to Jesus Christ. He understands the struggle we all endure. First Corinthians 10:13 says, "There hath no temptation taken you but such as is common to man; but God is faithful, who will not permit you to be tempted above that ye are able, but will, with the temptation, also make the way to escape, that ye may be able to bear it." Jesus Christ knows the path of victory over sin.

He Understood

The following story is told of a man named Booth Tucker, who was conducting evangelistic meetings in the great Salvation Army Citadel in Chicago. One night, after he had preached on the sympathy of Jesus, a man came forward and asked Mr. Tucker how he could talk about a loving, understanding, sympathetic God. "If your wife had just died, like mine has," the man said, "and your babies were crying for their mother—who will never come back—you wouldn't be saying what you're saying."

A few days later, Mr. Tucker's wife was killed in a train wreck. Her body was brought to Chicago and carried to the Citadel for the funeral. After the service the bereaved preacher looked down into the silent face of his wife and then turned to those who were attending. "The other day when I was here," he said, "a man told me that, if my wife had just died and my children were crying for their mother, I would not be able to say that Christ was understanding and sympathetic, or that He was sufficient for every need. If that man is here, I want to tell him that Christ is sufficient. My heart is broken; it is crushed, but it has a song, and Christ put it there. I want to tell that man that Jesus Christ speaks comfort to me today." The man was there, and he came and knelt beside the casket while Booth Tucker introduced him to Jesus Christ.

III. CHRIST'S PERFECT PROVISION (v. 16)

"Let us, therefore, come boldly unto the throne of grace, that we may obtain mercy, and find grace to help in time of need."

The author is exhorting the Hebrews who had given only mental assent to the gospel to come all the way to the throne of grace and obtain salvation. The throne of grace is God's throne.

It used to be a throne of judgment, but when Jesus sprinkled His blood upon it, He turned it into a throne of grace. That's His perfect provision.

What was it that sinful men needed? Mercy and grace. So we are to come boldly before God's throne to receive the grace He has provided for us through the perfect sacrifice of Jesus Christ. How can anyone reject such a High Priest? The phrase "find grace to help in time of need" means you will find grace when you need it most. And that time is now, before it's too late, and your heart is hard, and God's today is over.

Focusing on the Facts

1. What are some of the positive reasons the writer of Hebrews gives for receiving Jesus Christ (see p. 54)?
2. According to the parable of the sower, what causes people to make a false profession of faith in Christ (see p. 55)?
3. What is the theme of the book of Hebrews (see p. 56)?
4. What makes Jesus the perfect High Priest (see p. 56)?
5. On what basis did Jesus enter God's presence (see p. 57)?
6. Why is it significant that Jesus is sitting down in the Father's presence (see p. 58)?
7. True or false: It is not possible that a Christian could have any sins held against him. Give scriptural support for your answer (see p. 60).
8. Explain why we no longer need priests (see p. 60).
9. When Jesus died, the veil in the Temple that screened off the Holy of Holies was torn from top to bottom. What did that signify (see p. 60)?
10. What qualifies Jesus to be our sympathetic High Priest (see p. 61)?
11. What made Jesus' battle with temptation so much more difficult than ours (see p. 61)?
12. The Stoics believed that God's primary attribute was _____ (see p. 62).
13. True or false: The Epicureans believed the gods were actively involved in the affairs of this world and hence could sympathize with the struggles of men (see p. 62).
14. What does the Greek word translated "infirmities" in verse 15 mean (see pp. 62-63)?

15. How could Jesus understand our struggle with sin, since He Himself never sinned (see p. 63)?
16. What is the throne of grace (see pp. 64-65)?

Pondering the Principles

1. In the parable of the sower, Jesus mentioned four responses to the gospel. Three out of the four soils illustrate those who merely make an outward profession, not manifesting genuine saving faith. Many people in the church today give the outward appearance of being Christian but have never experienced true saving faith. In light of that sobering truth, examine the way you present the gospel to others. Do you stress what Jesus can do for people, or do you also warn them of the serious consequences of continuing in their sin and rejecting God? Note that the writer of Hebrews presented a balanced view of salvation throughout chapters 3 and 4. He not only stressed the benefits of coming to faith in Christ but also warned of the consequences if people fail to come to Him. If your presentation of the gospel lacks that balance, do a study of the gospels and Acts to see how Jesus and the apostles presented the gospel. Then pattern your own presentation after theirs.

2. In his book *The Knowledge of the Holy,* A. W. Tozer points out the importance of having our mental image of God correspond to how God has revealed Himself in the Bible. What comes into your mind when you think about God? Do you view Him as a stern, demanding parent ready to nail you the instant you step out of line? As a demanding coach for whom your performance is never quite good enough? As so utterly holy, He is unapproachable? As the Creator of the vast universe, indifferent to the affairs of men? The Bible does reveal God to be a holy, righteous judge who hates sin and will judge those sinners who fail to repent. God is the Creator of all the vast reaches of the universe. Yet the Bible also reveals that He is a gracious, loving, caring Father, who does not wish any to be lost (2 Pet. 3:9). As we learn from Hebrews 4:15, Jesus is a sympathetic, understanding High Priest. If you find your view of God to be inadequate, why not begin a study of His attributes? In addition to your Bible, you will find such books as Tozer's *The Knowledge of the Holy,* Arthur Pink's *The Attributes of God,* J. I. Packer's *Know-*

ing God, and Stephen Charnock's *The Existence and Attributes of God* to be of great value. You will never undertake a more important study.

Scripture Index

Topical Index